Real-World Writing
FOR TODAY'S KIDS

AGES 6-7

_____
Name

Writing: Tiffany Rivera
Lisa Vitarisi Mathews
Content Editing: Kathleen Jorgensen
Copy Editing: Cathy Harber
Art Direction: Yuki Meyer
Cover Design: Yuki Meyer
Design/Production: Jessica Onken
Yuki Meyer
Paula Acojido

EMC 6131

Evan-Moor®

Congratulations on your purchase of some of the finest teaching materials in the world.

No part of this book may be reproduced in any form or stored in any retrieval system without the written permission of publisher.

Evan-Moor Corporation
phone 1-800-777-4362, fax 1-800-777-4332.
Entire contents © 2021 Evan-Moor Corporation
18 Lower Ragsdale Drive, Monterey, CA 93940-5746. Printed in China.

CPSIA: Asia Pacific Offset Ltd, Kowloon, Hong Kong [11/2021]

CONTENTS

Real-World Writing for Today's Kids • EMC 6131 • © Evan-Moor Corp.

Welcome to Real-World Writing!

You already write every day, but writing isn't just for school. You write **notes to friends**. You **write on pictures** to say what things are or who people are. You **write silly songs**. You write your feelings, hopes, and dreams.

Writing will be part of your future, too. You can write your ideas and help other people. You can **write to solve problems**.

Words are powerful. They make people **feel** and **understand**. They can make the world better.

This book shows you different kinds of writing and gives you creative ways to practice doing your own writing.

Have fun!

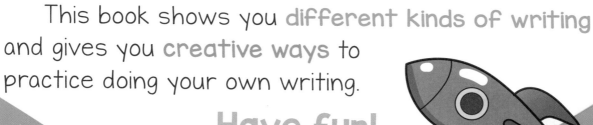

Journals Are About You!

These are journals. People write their thoughts and feelings in journals. They tell about what is happening in their lives.

June 20

We are on a trip. I met my cousin Ariana. She is 12 years old. She has a turtle named Shelly. Ariana is funny. She makes Shelly talk.

Hi. I'm Shelly!

June 21

Today we went to Navy Pier. We rode the big Ferris wheel. It went very high, but I wasn't scared. It was a sunny day. The lake was blue and calm. Later, we ate pizza. It was so good!

The person who wrote this journal writes about what she did each day.

April 9

I fed the ducks in the pond by the school bus stop. I like how they waddle and go "quack."

The person who wrote this journal likes to include a lot of drawings.

Real-World Writing for Today's Kids • EMC 6131 • © Evan-Moor Corp.

September 28

My friend across the street moved away. I am so sad! Now who will I ride bikes with after school? I already feel lonely and he has been gone for only three days.

September 30

I got a B on my math test! I am so happy!! I couldn't do word problems. Then my mom gave me some really fun ones to practice. I'm proud of myself!

The person who wrote this journal writes about how he feels.

Dear Diary,

We had fish for lunch today. I played jump rope with Sam and Terry at recess. They turned the rope faster, but I kept up!

I almost got a dog today! It followed me home from school. It's white with brown spots. It had a collar with a phone number. My parents called it, and they came and picked up the dog.

This person writes in a diary. A **diary** is another name for a journal. Some people start by writing "Dear Diary."

It's Your Life

Has your teacher ever asked you to draw a picture of yourself? Did you ever write to tell about yourself? Have you ever done "show-and-tell" at school? When you draw a picture of yourself, write about yourself, or do show-and-tell, you are sharing things about yourself.

A journal is different from these things because other people won't read it. It is just for you. You can write about your feelings. You can write about your day. You can write about things you like and things you don't like. A journal is a place to share whatever you want. Writing in a journal helps you think about your feelings.

October 12

Today was a fun day! I went to the skate park. I only fell two times!

Real-World Writing for Today's Kids • EMC 6131 • © Evan-Moor Corp.

When you write in a journal or a diary, you can do these things:

Write the date

Tell what happened during the day

Write how you feel

Draw pictures

Write what you worry about

Write what you hope will happen

Write about your friends

Write about your family

Write about or draw anything you want to

What's on Your Mind?

Your journal is a safe place for you to write about things that you are thinking about. Draw an **X** in the boxes next to what you might write about in your journal or diary.

- [ ] what happened at school today

- [ ] my family and my pets

- [ ] my friends

- [ ] what I like to do after school

- [ ] what I like to do on Saturday and Sunday

- [ ] what I am happy about

- [ ] what I am sad about or what I worry about

- [ ] what I want to be when I grow up

Real-World Writing for Today's Kids • EMC 6131 • © Evan-Moor Corp.

Pictures Show Who You Are

Some people draw pictures to tell about themselves or to show how they feel. Drawing pictures can be as important as writing words. What pictures tell about you? What might you draw in your journal or diary? Fill in the star next to the pictures that tell about you.

Write About a Day at School

Write a journal entry about a day at school. Tell about something that happened that you felt good about. Or tell about something that you did not feel good about. Draw a picture that shows how you felt about the day.

Date _____

_____

_____

_____

_____

_____

_____

_____

_____

_____

_____

_____

Write About Your Favorite Things

Write two journal entries about things you like.
Draw a picture in each shape.

_____

_____

_____

_____

_____

_____

_____

_____

_____

_____

_____

_____

_____

_____

Make a Journal

Make your own journal.

What You Need

- journal covers on page 15
- words and pictures on page 17
- large sheet of construction paper
- 10 sheets of white paper
- pencil or crayon
- scissors
- tape or glue
- stapler

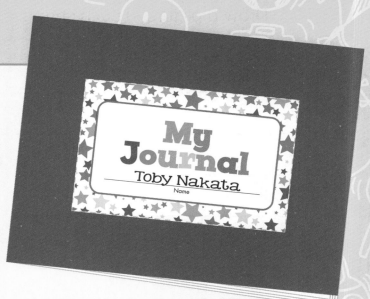

What You Do

1. Fold the construction paper to make the front cover and the back cover of your journal.

2. Choose which picture on page 15 you want to use for the front of your journal. Cut it out and tape or glue it onto the cover of your journal, or draw a picture of your own. Then write your name.

3. Look at the sheets of white paper. These are the pages for your journal. To decorate the pages, cut out the words or pictures on page 17. Then tape or glue them onto your journal pages.

4. Put the journal pages in between the front and back covers. Staple them together to make your journal.

Real-World Writing for Today's Kids • EMC 6131 • © Evan-Moor Corp.

My Journal

_____
Name

MY JOURNAL

_____
Name

What a Great Day!	**Not Happy!**
FUN WITH FRIENDS	**Happy!**
My Family	**Awesome!**
Not again!	**Something Funny**

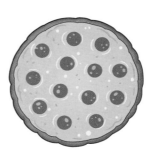

Congratulations

You've done important real-world writing!

You made a journal about YOU. Journals are a place to put your thoughts and feelings. Keeping a journal gives you a safe place to be you. If you like writing about and drawing your life, you may want one of these jobs one day:

Author

Illustrator

Blogger

Remember: Your feelings are important. It is good to think about your feelings. Writing in a journal helps you think about them.

Signs Help Us Know

These are door signs. Signs tell people many things.

This sign tells people that a grandma and grandpa live in this home.

David Calvert / Shutterstock.com

This sign tells people why they should stay out.

This sign tells people that they can come in and shop.

This sign uses pictures to tell people that they cannot bring food or drinks inside the room.

Read the Door

Signs are everywhere. You can see them along the road. You can see them at school. You can see them in stores. You can see them in your house, too! Many people put signs on their bedroom doors.

Welcome

Some bedroom signs have only pictures. This picture means "No girls allowed."

Some bedroom signs have words to tell people things.

Some signs have pictures and words.

QUIET PLEASE

Quiet Zone

A door sign should do these things:

- have one message

- have words or pictures or both

- be easy to read

- have colors that people will like

- be placed where people can see it

Your Room, Your Message

Bedroom door signs can have fun messages or can tell others what to do.
Draw an **X** next to the messages you might want on your bedroom door sign.

☐ **Quiet zone**

☐ **Let me sleep**

☐ **Come in**

☐ **Dog lovers only**

☐ **Please knock**

☐ **Say the password**

☐ **Kids only**

What You Might Draw

The colors and pictures on signs are an important part of getting people to see your message. Fill in the star below all the colors and pictures you'd like to see on a sign.

Two Door Signs

Think about what you would want to tell people before they open your bedroom door and go inside. Draw and write on the two bedroom door signs. One hangs on the door, and one hangs on the doorknob. Remember what a door sign should have on it.

A Sign for Your Bedroom Door

Make a door sign to hang on your bedroom doorknob!

What You Need

- doorknob sign on page 29
- pictures on page 31
- scissors
- tape or glue
- crayons or markers

What You Do

1. Cut out the doorknob sign on page 29. Cut along the dotted lines. Decide what you want your sign to say. What do you want people to know? What do you want them to see?

2. Look at the pictures and words on page 31. Decide if you want to use them to make your sign. If you do, cut them out and glue or tape them onto the doorknob sign.

3. Use crayons or markers to make your design. Then hang it on your doorknob.

Bonus

If you want to make a bigger sign, use a sheet of construction paper. Draw your design on it. Use a hole puncher to make two holes near the top end of the paper. Then put a piece of string through the holes and tie the ends together. Now your sign is ready to hang on your door!

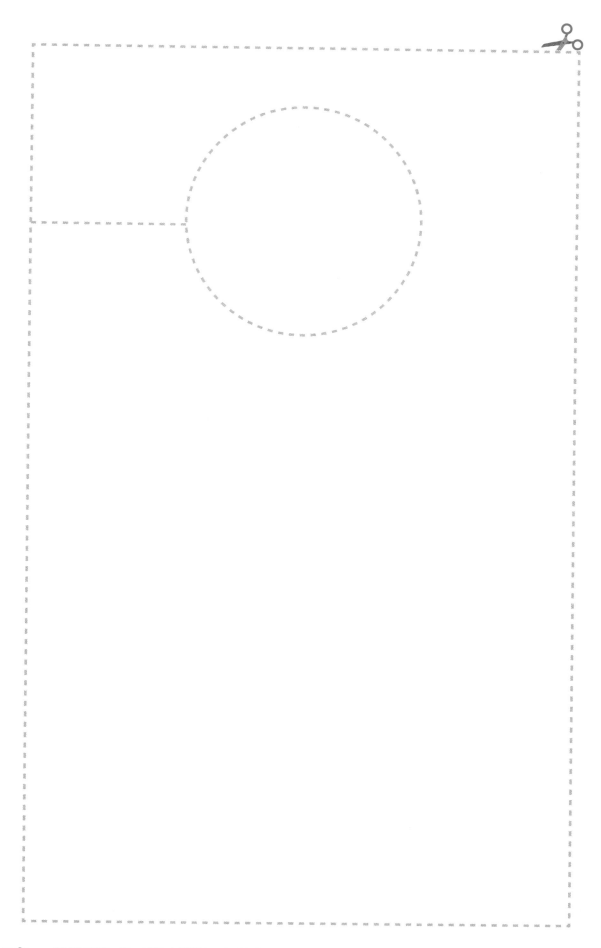

CONGRATULATIONS

You've done important real-world writing!

Signs are a good way to show and tell people a message. If you like making door signs, you may want one of these jobs one day:

Sign Maker

Graphic Designer

Web Designer

Remember: Your bedroom is a special place. You can tell people how you feel or what you need before they come into your bedroom. You can tell them if you need some alone time.

Chat with Your Class

This student goes to class online. He learns from his teacher using the computer. He can chat with his teacher by writing messages on a messenger app.

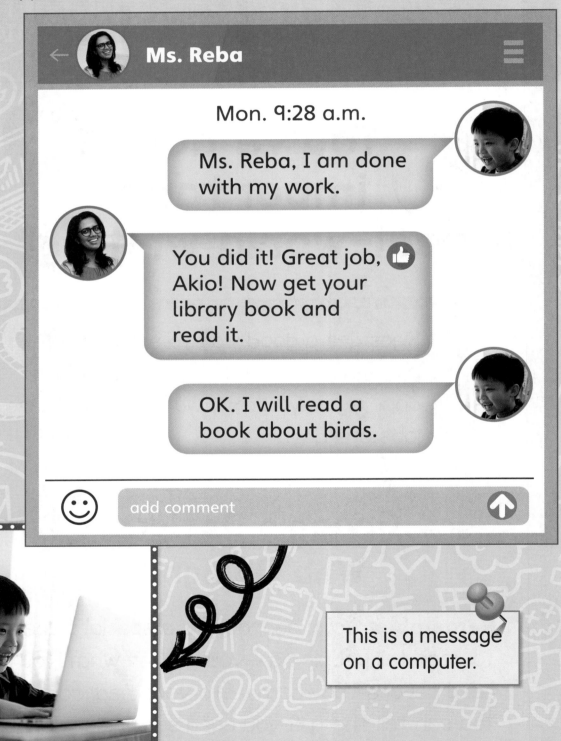

Ms. Reba

Mon. 9:28 a.m.

Ms. Reba, I am done with my work.

You did it! Great job, 👍 Akio! Now get your library book and read it.

OK. I will read a book about birds.

add comment

This is a message on a computer.

Wed. 2:05 p.m.

 Hi, class! I really liked your drawings.

 Thank you! I like your drawing, too. Your picture was funny. It made me laugh.

It was so much fun to draw!

☺ add comment ⬆

These students wrote messages to their classmates.

Messages in the Online Classroom

Some online classrooms use a messenger app. On a messenger app, students can chat or write messages to their teacher and classmates.

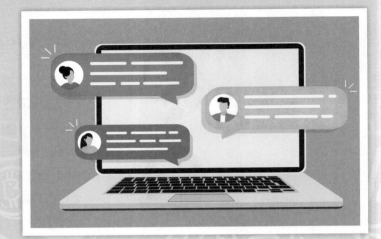

- 😊 You can write short or long messages.
- 😊 You can write important messages to your teacher about your work.
- 😊 You can write funny messages to your classmates.
- 😊 You can use emojis, or small pictures, in your messages to show how you feel.

Before you use an emoji, think about the person you are writing to. Think about what you are writing about. Remember, all messages you write should be kind.

Some teachers think students should not use emojis in important messages. They want students to use emojis only when talking to other students.

Ask your teacher about the rules for using emojis in your classroom.

Real-World Writing for Today's Kids • EMC 6131 • © Evan-Moor Corp.

An online message should have these things:

Good morning, teacher!

a greeting on your first comment or message

Hi, friend!

Hello, class!

a clear message

I read a book about a boy and a dog. I liked the story and the pictures.

pictures or emojis if your teacher says it is ok

It looks so yummy!

You are so cool!

important words

I need help.

Thank you!

kind words

Great job!

You did it!

Why You Would Write a Message

Students write messages to their teachers and classmates for many different reasons. Draw an **X** in the boxes next to the reasons why you might write a message.

☐ to ask a question

☐ to ask for help

☐ to tell about which assignments I finished

☐ to tell a classmate "Good job!"

☐ to tell what I think and feel about a story

☐ to say how I am feeling that day

☐ to say "Thank you"

☐ to tell what I like to do at home

Real-World Writing for Today's Kids • EMC 6131 • © Evan-Moor Corp.

Using Emojis and Pictures

Using emojis or pictures in a message can show others how you feel. Circle the emojis you would like to use in a message. Then fill in a star below each emoji to tell who would see it.

☆ teacher

☆ classmates

☆ teacher

☆ classmates

☆ teacher

☆ classmates

☆ teacher

☆ classmates

☆ teacher

☆ classmates

☆ teacher

☆ classmates

An Important Message

Pretend that you have an online classroom. Pretend that your teacher sent you the message below. Read what your teacher wrote. Then write in the chat bubble what you would say to your teacher.

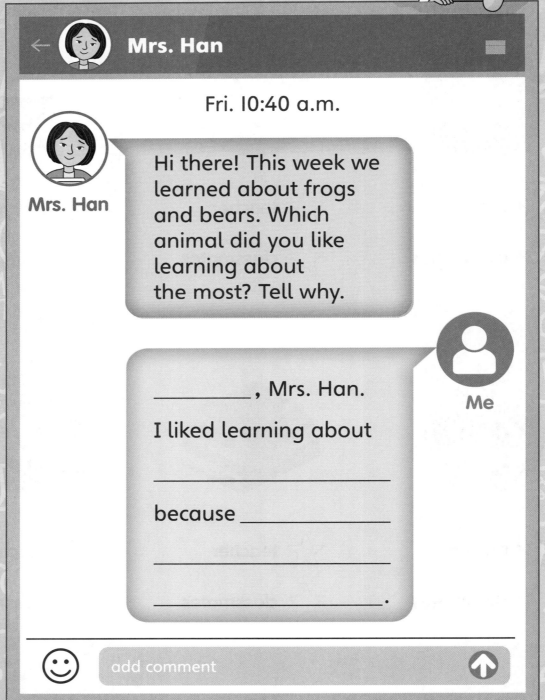

Mrs. Han

Fri. 10:40 a.m.

Mrs. Han

Hi there! This week we learned about frogs and bears. Which animal did you like learning about the most? Tell why.

Me

_____, Mrs. Han.

I liked learning about

_____

because _____

_____

_____.

add comment

A Fun Message

Pretend that you have an online classroom. Pretend that your friend sent you a message. Read what your friend wrote. Write in the chat bubble what you would say. Then draw the emojis or pictures you would use.

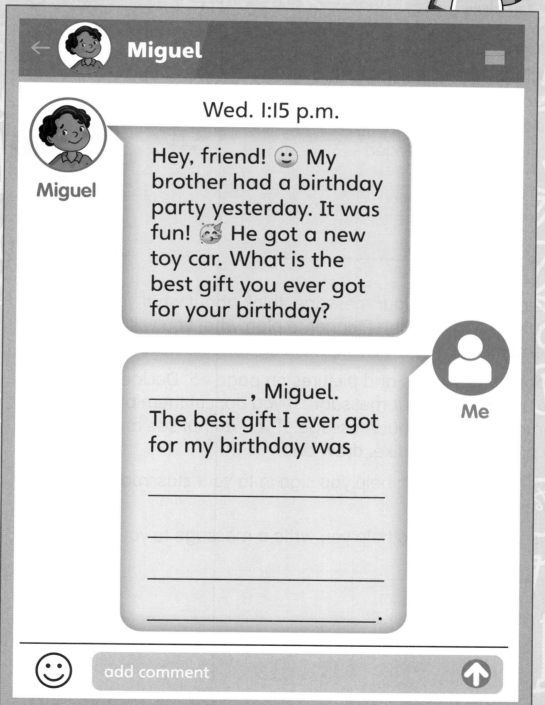

Miguel

Wed. 1:15 p.m.

Miguel

Hey, friend! 🙂 My brother had a birthday party yesterday. It was fun! 😹 He got a new toy car. What is the best gift you ever got for your birthday?

Me

_____ , Miguel. The best gift I ever got for my birthday was

_____

_____

_____

_____ .

🙂 add comment

A Message for Your Teacher

Have a grown-up help you write to your teacher using a messenger app. You can tell your teacher what you learned about writing an online message.

What You Need

- Planner on page 43
- Picture Cutouts on page 45
- pencil
- scissors
- tape or glue, if needed

What You Do

1. Before you write your message, think about what you learned. Write on the Planner to plan what you will write. Remember what an online message should have.

2. Look at the emojis and pictures on page 45. Decide if you want to use them in your message. If you do, cut them out and glue or tape them to your message. If you do not see an emoji or a picture that you like, draw one.

3. Ask a grown-up to help you sign in to your classroom's messenger app.

4. Use the Planner to help you write a message to your teacher.

PLANNER

Write in the chat bubbles to plan your message.

glue emoji here

_____ teacher,

I learned how to _____.

Some messages can be _____.

Some messages can be _____, too.

If I sent a classmate a message, I could use these emojis or pictures:

glue emoji here

glue emoji here

Is it okay if I send you emojis? I would like to send you these emojis in a message:

glue emoji here

glue emoji here

Picture Cutouts

Well Done!

You've done important real-world writing!

Online messages are a great way to talk to your teacher and classmates. If you like writing online messages, you may want one of these jobs one day:

Customer Service

Website Designer

Online Teacher

Remember: Think before you send a message. The words or pictures you use are important. Words can help people and they can hurt people. Use messages to help people.

A Special Message from You

These are greeting cards. People buy cards from a store or make them. People give cards to people for many reasons.

Yumi,

You are my very best friend. I hope your birthday is great!

Daisy

Many birthday cards have colorful pictures.

Dear Aunt Sophie,

I hope you are keeping warm in the snow!

Mom sent you cookies.

Love,

Kisha

Many people send holiday cards to let people know they are thinking of them on a special day or during a special season.

Ricky,

You did great on the spelling test! I am so happy for you!

Your friend,

Peter

"Congrats" is a short way to tell someone "Congratulations." It means that you are happy for that person.

I MISS YOU SO MUCH!

Some people send cards just to say "I miss you."

Dear Nana,

I wish I could see you more! You could help me practice soccer kicks.

Love,
Gina

Tayshaun,

I'm sorry I lost your game controller.

Your friend,

Josh

Sometimes it is hard to tell someone that you are sorry. A card can make it easier to tell someone you are sorry.

Special Wishes

Cards let you make a wish for someone you care about. You have probably seen cards with these wishes: Happy birthday! Get well soon! They can also tell people you are thinking about them: Good job! I miss you!

You can give cards for many reasons. You might make a card for someone who feels sad. You can give a card on a holiday such as Valentine's Day. You might give a card to someone who did something great. Getting a card feels good!

Many birthday cards have colorful pictures.

You can make a card at home or at school. When you make a card, it is extra special because there isn't another one like it!

A greeting card should have these things:

Pictures and words on the front of the card

Good Work!
I knew you
could do it!

A message on the inside of the card

Awesome job, Carrie!

Love,
Gramma

The name of the person you are giving it to and your name

WELCOME
to the WORLD

Pictures, colors, and decorations that help people know what the card is for

Words that tell how you feel or what the card is for

What Messages Do You Want to Share?

There are many reasons to send a card. One of the most important parts of a greeting card is the message. Draw an **X** in the boxes next to the messages you might send to your friends or your family.

- ☐ **Happy birthday to you!**
- ☐ **I'm sorry!**
- ☐ **I miss you!**
- ☐ **Good job!**

GOOD JOB!

What holidays does your family celebrate? Write two of the names. Then write your own holiday messages.

Holiday _____

Message _____

_____

Holiday _____

Message _____

_____

Pictures Say a Lot!

Greeting cards have different colors and pictures. The colors and pictures help people know what the card is for. Fill in the star below all the colors and pictures you'd like to see on a greeting card.

Practice Making a Card

Before you make a card, think about what you want it to say and look like. Write and draw in the boxes below to plan your card.

What message will you write on the front of the card?

What picture will you draw on the front?

What will you write on the inside of the card?

Now that you've planned your practice card, draw and write below to show what it will look like.

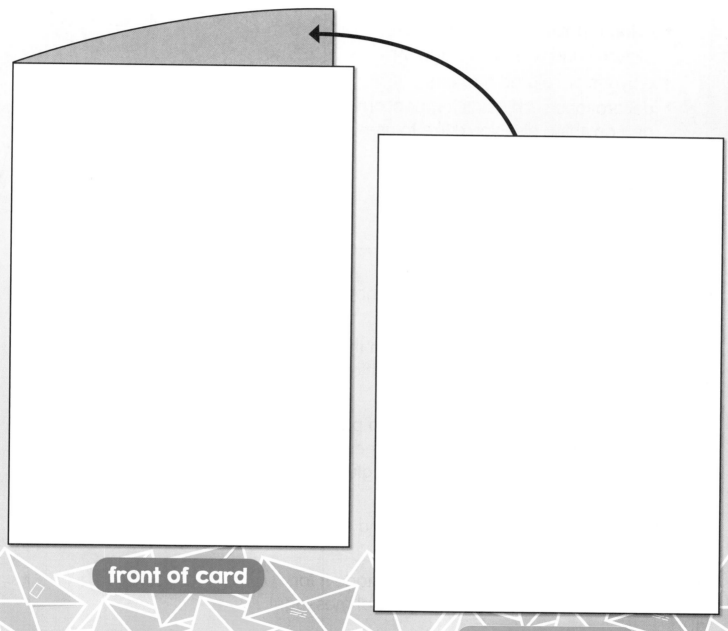

front of card

inside of card

Make a Card

Make a card with a special message for a family member or a friend!

What You Need

- colored paper on the next page
- pictures and words on page 59
- crayons or colored markers
- decorations such as glitter, popcorn, stickers, and anything else you'd like to use
- scissors
- tape or glue

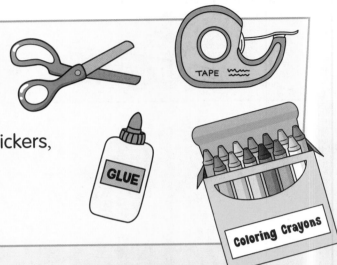

What You Do

1. Decide who the card is for and what you want it to say.

2. Tear out the paper for the card on the next page and fold it in half. Decide which way you will make your card.

3. Look at the words and pictures on page 59 and decide if you want to use any of them on your card. If you do, cut them out and glue or tape them to your card.

4. Use colored markers, crayons, and other decorations to make your card.

5. Give the card to the person you made it for. Watch him or her read your special message!

Real-World Writing for Today's Kids • EMC 6131 • © Evan-Moor Corp.

fold

Get well Soon!

Happy HOLIDAYS!

Well Done!

You've done important real-world writing!

You made a card for someone special to you! Greeting cards are a great way to show people that you are thinking of them. If you like writing special messages and drawing pictures, you may want one of these jobs one day:

Greeting Card Writer

Poet   **Artist**

Remember: Your words and your pictures are special. Telling people how you feel can make you and the person you tell feel good!

Do It Your Way

These are persuasive letters. People write letters like this to get someone to do something or to agree with them.

Dear Principal Chen,

    Recess is too short. It should be more than 30 minutes. We need more time to play. When kids play, kids learn things like how to be a good friend. A longer recess gives my teacher a longer break, too. Everyone will be more happy. This is why I think recess should be longer.

Thank you,
Trey

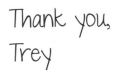

This boy wrote a letter to the school principal. He thinks recess should be longer. Trey wants Principal Chen to make it longer.

Hello Mommy,

I really want to go to Sherita's birthday party. Sherita is my best friend. We will play games and ride a pony. You can come to the party, too. You can make sure that I am safe on the pony. Please let me go. It will be a lot of fun.

Love,
Gabby

Gabby's friend is having a birthday party. Gabby wants to go. She wrote her mom a letter to get her to agree.

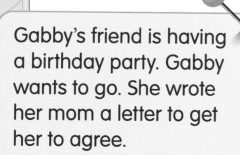

Why You Should Say "Yes"

People write persuasive letters to ask someone for something they want. For example, Pablo wants his parents to get him a pet. He wrote them a letter telling them all the reasons that it is a good idea. That is a persuasive letter. Sandy wants Ana to like her favorite game. She wrote Ana a letter telling her all the reasons why she should like the game. That is a persuasive letter.

Before you write a persuasive letter, think about who the letter is for. Think about why that person may say "no" to what you ask for. The letter should make the person think or feel the same way you do.

Dear Mr. Rico,

    I am happy that our class won an ice cream party. But I can't eat ice cream. Could we have a painting party? We can paint what we want. Everyone can do it. And we can keep our art after the party! Please think about my idea.

Love,
Dev

A persuasive letter should have these things:

a greeting

Hi Luna,

a sentence that tells what you want

I think we should play with blocks when you come over to my house. We should play with blocks because there are many fun things to do with them. We can make a tall tower. We can make a barn for our toy animals. We can make a house for your dolls, too! **It will be so fun.** I can't wait to play with you!

reasons why you feel the way you do

reasons that may make the person want to say "yes"

kind words

Love,
Apollo

a closing

Letters You Would Write

People write persuasive letters to different people for many reasons. Draw an **X** next to the things you might want. Then draw an **X** next to the people you would write a persuasive letter to.

You want

- [ ] a pet
- [ ] a new toy
- [ ] a long recess
- [ ] new books
- [ ] to choose what to eat for dinner
- [ ] to be on a team or part of a group
- [ ] to go to a special place

You will ask

- [ ] Mom
- [ ] Dad
- [ ] a grandparent
- [ ] a brother
- [ ] a sister
- [ ] a friend
- [ ] a teacher

Pictures That Persuade

Using colors and pictures make a letter fun to read. Fill in the star below all the colors and pictures you'd like to see in your letter.

Persuasive Letter to Your Family

Pretend that you and your family are planning a fun day together. You want to swim at the beach. But your family wants to hike in the woods. Finish the letter to someone in your family to change his or her mind.

Dear _____,

I want to swim at the beach on our family fun day. We should go to the beach and not the woods. Here are 3 reasons why:

1. _____

_____

2. _____

_____

3. _____

_____

We will have the best day ever at the beach!

Love,

_____

Persuasive Letter to Your Friend

Pretend that you and a friend are having a sleepover. Your friend wants to play with puzzles. But you want to play with something else. Think about what you want to play with. Finish the sentences to get your friend to agree with you.

Hi _____,

I think we should play _____
at our sleepover. Here are 3 reasons why:

1. _____

   _____

2. _____

   _____

3. _____

   _____

We will have so much fun!

Your friend,

_____

Ask for What You Need

Write a letter to ask someone for something you need!

What You Need

- Planner on page 71
- Picture Cutouts on page 73
- sheet of paper
- pencil
- scissors
- tape or glue, if needed

What You Do

1. First, think about what you need. Think about who you will write the letter to. Write these on the Planner.

2. Now think about your reasons. Think about what the person reading your letter might say. Write a few words on the Planner so you remember.

3. Use the Planner to write your letter on a sheet of paper.

4. Look at the words and pictures on page 73. Decide if you want to use them in your letter. If you do, cut them out. Tape or glue them to your letter.

5. Give your letter to the person you wrote to. See if your letter made them say "yes" to you! Good luck!

Real-World Writing for Today's Kids • EMC 6131 • © Evan-Moor Corp.

Use the planner to plan what you will write.

What I want _____

Who I will write to _____

Reason 1	Reason 2	Reason 3

Why the person might say "no."

Why the person should say "yes."

Picture Cutouts

CONGRATULATIONS

You've done important real-world writing!

Persuasive letters are a good way to ask people for what you want. Persuasive letters are a good way to get someone to think the same way you do. If you like writing persuasive letters, you may want one of these jobs one day:

Lawyer

Salesperson

TV Commercial Writer

Remember: If you want something, ask for it. But if a person says "no," you can still be kind. Just say to yourself, "Maybe next time."

How to Take Care of a Pet

People have many different kinds of pets.
Different pets need different kinds of food and care.

How to Care for Squeaky

The person who wrote these directions has a pet bird. It needs the same care each day.

Clean cage: Change the paper on the bottom of Squeaky's cage each day.

Food and water: Clean the water holder and put fresh water in it each day. Fill the food bowl with seeds when it is almost empty.

Play time: Let Squeaky out of his cage every day for three hours. Talk to him.

Scooter's Schedule

Sunday	Clean Scooter's tank. Take out the old water and pour clean water in it. Feed Scooter some pellets.
Tuesday	Take Scooter out of her tank and put her outside in the sun for 1 hour. Feed her fresh lettuce.
Thursday	Change Scooter's tank water and give her dried worms.
Saturday	Take Scooter out of her tank and put her outside in the sun for 1 hour. Feed her fresh lettuce.

This person's turtle needs care only every other day.

When and How to Feed Rufus

8:00 a.m.

Let Rufus out in the backyard. Clean his water bowl and food bowl.

Pour a cup of dog food into his food bowl and fill up his water bowl.

12:00 p.m.

Play with Rufus outside. Give him a treat.

5:00 p.m.

Feed Rufus a cup of dog food and give him more water.

The person who wrote these directions has a dog. The schedule shows what to do each day at different times.

Taking Care of Boots

Morning: Put 1 can of food in the cat's bowl. The cans are in a stack next to the bowl. Wash the bowl after she eats.

Put fresh water in her water bowl.

Night: Put 1 scoop of dry food in the cat's bowl. The food is in a bag next to the cans.

Put more water in her water bowl.

This person's cat needs food and water in the morning and at night.

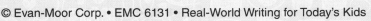

Pets Need Care

Writing directions for how to care for a pet is an important job. Pets need food, water, and a safe place to be. Different pets need different kinds of care. For example, birds need a clean cage and dogs need to be walked. Sometimes the same kind of pet needs care in different ways. For example, some dogs sleep outside and some sleep inside. Some cats want to play when they wake up, and some want to eat first.

Caring for Sunny

Thank you for taking care of our fish, Sunny.

Monday: Feed her fish flakes and lettuce.

Wednesday: Feed her fish flakes. Take out the old lettuce.

Friday: Take out four cups of water. Don't take out Sunny! Pour in four cups of fresh water. Feed her fish flakes.

Sunday: Feed her fish flakes and worm treats!

Pet-care directions should have these things:

what you want the person to do

the things they need to use

the steps the person should follow

what time things need to be done

pictures that tell more about what you want done

What Do They Need to Know?

There are many parts to pet care. Some parts are feeding, walking, playing, and cleaning. Draw an **X** next to all the things that you should put in your directions. Then write anything else you think of.

☐ when to feed your pet and give it water

☐ how and when to give your pet exercise

☐ when to clean up after your pet

☐ where to find the pet supplies and food

☐ how and when to clean your pet

☐ how to contact your pet's vet

☐ _____

☐ _____

 Real-World Writing for Today's Kids • EMC 6131 • © Evan-Moor Corp.

What Different Pets Need

People have many different kinds of pets. Each pet needs different things for its care. Which animal do you have or would you like to have as a pet? Fill in the circle below it. Then fill in the stars below the pictures that show what that pet may need for its care.

Class Pet

Pretend that your class decided to get a pet for the classroom. They chose a hamster. Everyone helps take care of it. Read the pet-care directions. Mark all the things you'd like to do to take care of the class hamster.

How to Take Care of Mr. Furry

☐ **Change the hay in Mr. Furry's cage once each week.**
Take Mr. Furry out of his cage and put him in his rolling ball. Put the rolling ball on the floor. Have someone watch him. Take out the old hay. Wipe the bottom of the cage with a paper towel. Put in clean hay. Put Mr. Furry back in, too.

☐ **Feed Mr. Furry every morning.**
Get the bag of hamster food. Put a cup of food in Mr. Furry's bowl.

☐ **Give Mr. Furry clean water every day.**
Take the water bottle out of the cage. Empty it and fill it with clean water. Put it back in the cage.

☐ **Play with Mr. Furry for 30 minutes each day.**
Take Mr. Furry out of his cage. Go to a quiet place and gently pet him. Then put him in his rolling ball and let him roll around in it. Watch him closely!

 Real-World Writing for Today's Kids • EMC 6131 • © Evan-Moor Corp.

Hamster Pet-Care Directions

Pretend that you are going away to camp. Your sister will take care of your hamster, Hammy. Make a schedule that tells her what to do.

When to feed Hammy:

What to feed Hammy:

When to fill Hammy's water:

How to clean Hammy's cage:

How to play with Hammy:

Please Take Care of This Pet

Write pet-care directions for a pet that you have. If you do not have a pet, ask a family member or a friend if you can write pet-care directions for a pet he or she has.

What You Need

- Planner on page 85
- Pet-Care Directions form on page 87
- pencil or pen
- crayons or markers

What You Do

1. Choose a pet to write pet-care directions for.

2. Use the Planner to plan what you will write. If you are writing directions for someone else's pet, take the Planner with you when you talk to the pet's owner.

3. Use the Planner to write the pet-care directions on the Pet-Care Directions form.

4. Draw pictures of the things that are needed to take care of the pet. Draw the pet.

5. If you wrote about a pet you have, keep the directions and use them when you need them. If you wrote pet-care directions for someone else's pet, give the pet owner the directions to keep.

PLANNER

Name of pet

Picture of pet

Things you need

What to feed it

Where to find the food

When to feed it

Vet's name

PET-CARE DIRECTIONS FOR

_____
pet's name

Congratulations!

You've done important real-world writing!

You wrote pet-care directions. Writing pet-care directions is an important job. You can keep animals safe and healthy by writing pet-care directions for the people who are caring for them. If you like writing pet-care directions, you may want one of these jobs one day:

Veterinarian

Horse Trainer

Pet Store Worker

Remember: The pet-care directions you write are important. They can help keep a pet healthy, happy, and safe.

A Message for Your Neighbors

These are yard signs. People put signs in their yards to tell their neighbors something.

This sign was made to thank community helpers in the neighborhood.

© Rosemarie Mosteller / Shutterstock.com

YOU MAKE M HAPPY WHEN SKIES ARE GRAY

© lev radin / Shutterstock.com

This sign was made to make people smile as they drive by.

 Real-World Writing for Today's Kids • EMC 6131 • © Evan-Moor Corp.

People made this sign to cheer on their neighbors.

This sign tells the people walking by that no dogs are allowed on the lawn.

Say It on a Sign

© Pocket Canyon Photography / Shutterstock.com

People make yard signs to tell their neighbors something. There are many different reasons for making yard signs. Some people want to thank people who helped during a fire or a flood. Some people want to tell people that they did a good job finishing school. Some people want to tell people the rules of their house or what they think. Some people just want to make people smile as they pass by.

Some yard signs have words. Some have pictures. Some have both. All yard signs are placed where other people can see them. People who don't have a yard can place a sign in a window.

A yard sign should have these things:

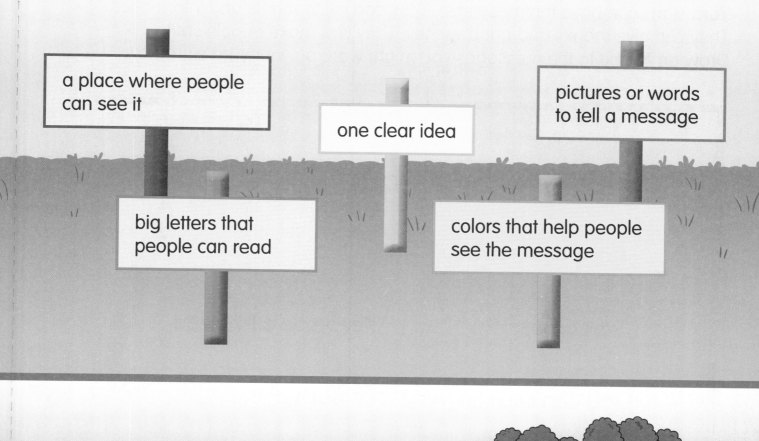

a place where people can see it

one clear idea

pictures or words to tell a message

big letters that people can read

colors that help people see the message

Message Ideas

Yard signs can have fun messages. They can tell thoughts and information. They can give thanks and good wishes. They can make people smile. Draw an **X** next to the messages you might want on your yard sign.

- ☐ Thank you, firefighters
- ☐ Have a great day!
- ☐ Welcome!
- ☐ You can do it !
- ☐ Peace!
- ☐ Be kind
- ☐ Be yourself
- ☐ Keep our city clean
- ☐ Be safe
- ☐ Animal lovers live here

You are loved!

Colors and Pictures to Stand Out

Using colors and pictures on a yard sign can make people want to look at and read your message. Fill in the star below all the colors and pictures you'd like to see on your sign.

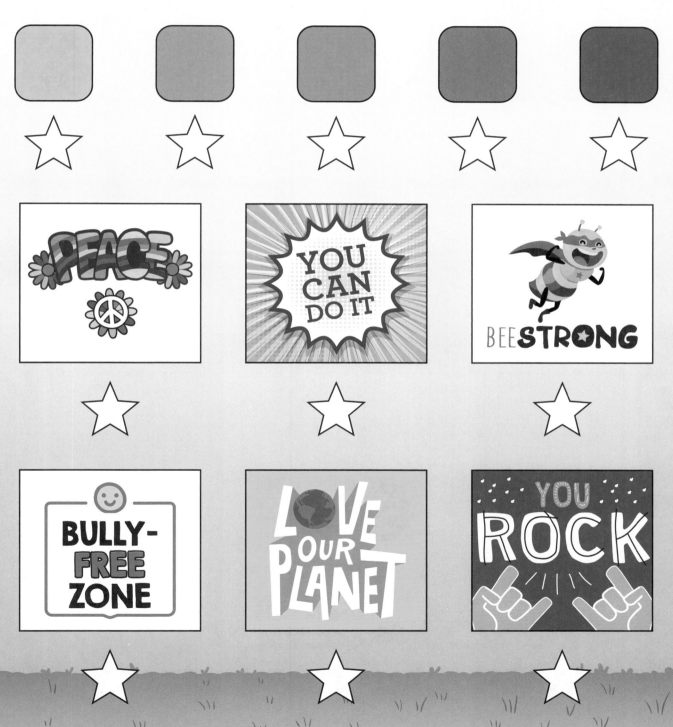

A Yard Sign to Welcome New Neighbors

Pretend that new families have moved onto your street. Draw pictures and write words on a sign to welcome them to the neighborhood.

A Yard Sign for a Clean Neighborhood

Pretend that you have seen trash on the ground. Draw pictures and write words that will make people want to keep the neighborhood clean.

Your Own Yard Sign

Make a sign of your own. Work with your family to plan and make a yard sign to place in your front yard or in a window.

What You Need

- Planner on page 99
- Picture Cutouts on page 101
- piece of cardboard or poster board
- pencil
- markers or paint
- decorating supplies such as construction paper, glitter, scissors, and glue (optional)

What You Do

1. Ask a family member to help you plan and make a yard sign. Use the Planner to plan your sign. Remember what a yard sign should have.

2. Copy the design you made on the Planner onto the cardboard or poster board.

3. Decorate your sign. You can cut out pictures from the Picture Cutouts page and glue them onto your sign. You can also use markers, paint, and other supplies, if you'd like.

4. When you are done, place the sign in your yard or in a window where people outside can see it.

Planner

Use this page to draw and write your yard sign idea. Then copy your design onto cardboard or poster board.

Picture Cutouts

YOU DID IT

You've done important real-world writing!

Yard signs are a good way to tell your neighbors a message. If you like making yard signs, you may want one of these jobs one day:

Sign Maker   **Book Illustrator**

Ad Writer

Remember: The words and pictures you use are powerful. They can make people think and feel. Think before you say, draw, or write something. Always be kind!

Let's Help Others

These are fundraising letters. People write fundraising letters to ask for money to do something good. Fundraising letters make someone want to help you.

> An animal shelter needs more money to feed its animals. Matt wrote a fundraising letter to ask for help.

Dear Mrs. Tanna,

My name is Matt. I live next door. My dad and I help out at the animal shelter every weekend. They just got a lot more animals after the forest fire. They need more money to feed them all.

My goal is to give the shelter $100 on Saturday. I am asking everyone I know. Can you give a little money? You can bring it to our house any day this week. The animals will say "thank you!"

Your neighbor,
Matt

Real-World Writing for Today's Kids • EMC 6131 • © Evan-Moor Corp.

Vera's baseball team needs money for a bus. She wrote a fundraising letter to ask a restaurant owner for help.

Dear Mr. Richards,

My name is Vera. I am on the Eagles baseball team. We eat pizza at your restaurant after every game. But now we need your help. Our team has to win one more game to become the champion! But the game is far away. We need $500 to rent a bus.

Can you help us go to our last game? Please give any amount of money. Send it to our website: www.eaglesbaseball.com by March 19. If you give $500, we will put "Ric's Pizza" on our uniforms!

Thank you for helping our team.

Sincerely,
Vera

It's Good to Give

People write fundraising letters to ask for help for people or groups who need things. Many fundraising letters ask for money. Here are some things people need money for:

food

supplies

services

Before you write a fundraising letter, think about what the money is for. Think about what you can say to get people to help.

Dear neighbor,

Do your kids play at the Elm City Playground? I do, but my sister, Lily, can't. She uses a wheelchair. She can't go on the slide or the swings. My family is raising money to make the playground fun for everyone. We want to add things that Lily can play on.

We need $1,000 by this summer.
If you can give a little, it will add up.

Thank you,
Carlos and Lily

A fundraising letter should say these things:

Dear friends,

I learned that many kids in Haiti don't have shoes. It rains a lot there. They can't go to school without shoes. They need shoes!

why you are writing the letter

I am collecting money for them. My dad will send them all the money I collect so they can buy shoes. I want to get $100.

what you need

what your goal is

Please give me your money by March 31. Your money will help kids in Haiti go to school and keep their feet safe.

the last day to give

why someone should help

Thank you,
Latif

who you are

Fundraising Ideas

People write fundraising letters for many reasons. Draw an **X** next to the things you might need. Then draw an **X** next to the people you would ask.

I want to raise money for

- [ ] books for my class
- [ ] a field trip
- [ ] meals for the needy
- [ ] a classroom party

I will ask

- [ ] family
- [ ] friends
- [ ] neighbors
- [ ] shop owners

Real-World Writing for Today's Kids • EMC 6131 • © Evan-Moor Corp.

Art to Get Noticed

Colors and pictures make others want to read your letter. They can help convince people to give. Fill in the star below all the colors and pictures you might use in your letter.

School Garden

Pretend that your school wants to start a garden. Finish the sentences in the letter. It should ask someone to give money for seeds and tools.

Dear _____,

My name is _____.

I am a student at _____.

We need a garden so we can _____

_____.

My school needs $_____ to buy _____.

You should give money because _____

_____

You can bring your money to the office.

Thank you for helping my school.

    Sincerely,

_____

City Library

Pretend that your library was flooded in a bad storm. The rugs and the books got all muddy! They can't be cleaned. Finish the sentences in the letter. It should ask someone to give money for new rugs and books.

Dear _____,

My name is _____.

I live in _____.

Our city library was _____.

We need to buy new _____.

Any money you give will let us _____

_____.

Please send any money to the _____

City Library before _____.

Thank you for your help!

    Sincerely,

    _____

Ask for Help

Write your own fundraising letter to ask someone for help.

What You Need

- Planner on page 113
- fundraising letter on page 115
- pencil

What You Do

1. First, think about what you would like to raise money for. Who needs something important? Whom will you ask to help? Talk to a grown-up to make sure it is okay to ask for help.

2. Use the Planner to decide what you will write in your letter. Remember what a fundraising letter should have.

3. Write your letter on the fundraising letter page. Use your Planner to help you.

4. Give your letter to someone who can help.

Planner

Use this page to write down ideas for your fundraising letter.

Why are you writing this letter?	
Who needs help?	
Why do they need help?	
How can people help?	
Why should people help?	

Dear _____,

My name is _____.

I am writing to you because _____

_____

_____.

This is important because _____

_____

_____.

You can help by _____.

Your gift will help _____

_____.

The last day to help is _____.

Thank you for your help and kindness!

        Sincerely,

        _____

FANTASTIC!

You've done important real-world writing!

Fundraising letters are a good way to ask people for help. If you like writing fundraising letters, you may want one of these jobs one day:

Fundraiser

Volunteer

TV Commercial Writer

Remember: Everyone needs help sometimes. Helping one person helps us all. If you ever need help, be sure to ask someone.

This Toy Is Fun!

These are toy reviews. People write toy reviews to tell other people what they think about a toy. They put them on websites for other people to read.

https://...

Busy Blocks Toy Review
by Maddie Rae

okay   good   best

Busy Blocks has many different shapes of blocks. I like this toy because there are a lot of ways to play with it.

You can make a big shape with many little shapes. You can put all the shapes with the same color together. You can count the shapes.

I think all kids should play with this toy. Busy Blocks is fun to play with and helps you learn!

Some people read their toy reviews in front of a camera. This child made a video. It tells why he likes to play with his toy airplane.

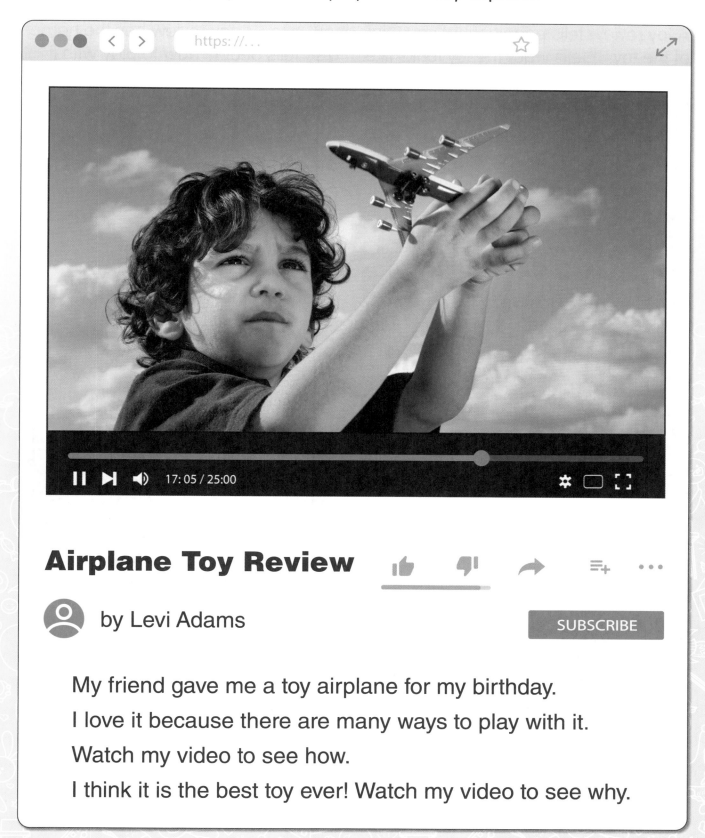

Airplane Toy Review 👍 👎 ➡ ≡₊ •••

👤 by Levi Adams

SUBSCRIBE

My friend gave me a toy airplane for my birthday.

I love it because there are many ways to play with it.

Watch my video to see how.

I think it is the best toy ever! Watch my video to see why.

This Is What I Think!

A toy review tells people what you think about a toy. A toy review has the name of the toy. It tells what the toy looks like. It also tells people how to play with it. If it is a game, it tells how many people can play it. The person writing the toy review tells if they like the toy or not.

Some people write a review to say how they feel about a toy.

Some people record their toy review on a phone or a camera.

Then they show it to someone.

A toy review should say these things:

My aunt gave me some money to buy any toy I wanted. I bought a pair of walkie talkies. They look kind of like phones, but they only call each other.

Al and I used the walkie talkies outside. You push a button and say something and let go. Then the other person does that, too.

It was fun, but they stopped working. Mom said the batteries died. I don't think you should buy this toy. It didn't last very long.

the name of the toy

what the toy looks like

how to play with the toy

if he or she likes the toy and why

if a friend should buy this toy

What Do You Want to Know?

A toy review tells many things about a toy. Toy reviews help other people decide if they want to buy it. Pretend that you might buy a toy that you heard about. What do you want to know about that toy? Draw an **X** in the boxes next to what you want to know about the toy.

- [ ] what color the toy is
- [ ] how to play with the toy
- [ ] if you and a friend can play with it together
- [ ] if the toy is easy to play with
- [ ] if the toy is fun to play with
- [ ] if the toy helps you learn

Real-World Writing for Today's Kids • EMC 6131 • © Evan-Moor Corp.

Toy Review for a Learning Toy

Think about all your toys. Choose one toy that helps you learn. Write a review. Draw the toy. Color the face to show how much you like it. Then complete the sentences to tell more about the toy.

_____ Review

toy name

by _____

your name

Draw the toy.

I don't like this toy.

I like this toy.

It's the best toy!

This toy helps you learn about _____

_____.

I like this toy because _____

_____.

Video Toy Review

You practiced writing a toy review. Now make a video toy review. You will plan what to say. Then you will read it into a phone, a camera, or a computer.

What You Need

- Planner on page 125
- My Toy Review on page 127
- pencil
- phone, camera, or computer to record your video
- the toy or a picture of it

What You Do

1. Pick a toy to talk about. Use the Planner to think about what you want to say. Write to finish all the parts of the Planner.

2. Use the Planner to write your toy review on page 127. Finish the sentences at the top. Then keep writing!

3. Practice reading your review out loud.

4. Ask a grown-up to record you as you read your review. Be sure to look at the camera and show the toy or a picture of the toy.

5. Then show your video to a friend or a family member.

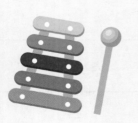

Real-World Writing for Today's Kids • EMC 6131 • © Evan-Moor Corp.

Planner

Use this page to plan your toy review.

Toy name:

Circle to finish the sentence:

I play with it _____.   by myself   with a friend

What I do with it:

What I **like** about this toy:

Why:

What I **don't like** about this toy:

Why:

Fill in the row of stars to tell what you think.

	I don't like this toy.
	I like this toy.
	You should buy this toy!

My Toy Review

Hi! My name is _____.

I am going to tell you about

_____.

First, I will show it to you.

When I play with this toy, _____

_____

_____

_____

_____

_____.

CONGRATULATIONS

You've done important real-world writing!

Writing reviews and making videos are great ways to tell people how you feel about something. If you like writing reviews and making videos, you may want one of these jobs one day:

Blogger

Actor

Writer

Remember: Some people like the same things as you. Other people do not like the same things as you. And that is okay. How you feel matters. How other people feel matters, too. Be kind when saying how you feel.